P9-AGN-893

CATS

By Elsa Posell

TABLE OF CONTENTS

Scott

℗ CHILDRENS PRESS, CHICAGO

Both the tiger and the house cat have soft pads on their feet.
They can move and run without making a sound.

THE CAT FAMILY

Can you believe that lions and tigers, leopards and cheetahs, jaguars, mountain lions, ocelots, and lynx all belong to the cat family?

These cats live in different places. They are not the same size or color. But there are many things about cats that are the same. All cats eat meat.

A house cat purrs when
it is happy. So does the
puma, lynx, bobcat, and
ocelot. Lions and tigers
cannot purr; they roar.
Jaguars and leopards
make coughing or barking
sounds.

LIONS

The lion lives in Africa. The male lion is larger than the female. Only the male has a mane of long hair.

Lions have very strong jaws. They can kill a zebra or an antelope with one sharp bite. They are very fast and can jump long distances.

Lions sleep as much as nineteen hours a day.

Right: Lion cub has all its teeth when it is three months old.
Below: Sleeping male

When the sun sets, they hunt for food. Often lions hunt in groups of four or eight.

A mother lion has from two to four babies, called cubs. At birth, their fur is spotted. Cubs drink their mother's milk.

Baby lions are very playful. When the babies are one-and-one-half years old, the mother lion begins to teach them to hunt.

TIGERS

Tigers live in jungle swamps or tall grasses of Asia. One kind lives in Siberia.

Tigers are stronger and larger than lions. They are very smart and brave.

They hunt for food at night. Only when a tiger is very hungry will it look for food when it is light.

Tigers can swim and climb

Above left: Siberian tiger
Above: Twelve-week-old Bengal tiger
Below: Tigers playing in water

trees when they have to. They can also jump as high as fifteen feet. The tiger often hunts alone.

A mother tiger has from three to five cubs or kittens. She takes good care of them. They stay close to their mother and drink her milk.

Cubs stay with their mother for about two years. They are full grown when they are four years old.

LEOPARDS

Leopards live in the forests of Asia and Africa. They are very fast runners, good tree climbers, and good jumpers. Leopards hunt at night.

The mother leopard has from two to four cubs or kittens. She teaches them to hunt and to watch out for enemies. Leopards are full grown when they are three years old.

Snow leopard

CHEETAHS

The cheetah is also called the hunting leopard. It is so easy to tame that hunters can train it to catch animals for them.

The cheetah is tall with long legs. It can run as

fast as seventy miles an hour for short distances.

Cheetahs can jump as high as twenty feet. They are found in Asia and Africa. Cheetahs hunt in pairs or in small groups. Before hunting, they always sharpen their claws on a tree.

JAGUARS

The jaguar is found in the wilds of Mexico and South America. In many ways, the jaguar looks like a leopard. It, too, is light yellow with dark, circlelike spots.

Left: Seven-week-old jaguar
Below: Black jaguar

Jaguars hunt wild animals on the ground. They also go into water to catch fish, turtles, and water snakes. They will climb trees when they are hungry.

The mother jaguar has two to four cubs. The father jaguar looks after the babies while the mother hunts for food.

LYNX

The lynx has a thick coat of fur.

Snowshoe rabbits are its favorite food. But when it is hungry it will eat squirrels, mice, foxes, and other small animals.

Canada lynx

PUMAS

Pumas are found in South America and North America. Pumas are also called mountain lions, cougars, and sometimes even panthers.

The mother has two to four kittens who are born

Puma or mountain lion

Three-week-old cubs
with their mother

with dark spots over their
fur. These spots go away
as the cubs grow older.
Cubs stay with their
mother until they are about
two years old and can
hunt for their own food.

Ocelots have dark markings on their heads, necks, and bodies.

OCELOTS

Ocelots live in the forests of North and South America. They look so much like small tigers that they have at times been called leopard or tiger cats.

Ocelots eat rats, mice, snakes, lizards, and other small animals. When very hungry they may climb trees to find birds and other animals.

BOBCATS

Bobcats are found in
North America. They are
shy animals and are not
seen often. The color of

the fur of these wild cats differs in different parts of the country.

Swamps, forests, deserts, and mountains are home to the bobcats. They are good hunters. Rabbits are their favorite food, but they can climb trees to get birds and other small animals.

THE CAT
COMES TO MAN

Many years ago, all animals were wild. People tamed some of them to work for them or to be pets. The cat was one of the last to be tamed.

Cats make very good pets. They are very clean. They need less care than other animals.

KINDS OF CATS

There are long-haired
cats and short-haired cats.
Long-haired cats are
lovely to look at. Their soft
silky fur needs to be
brushed often.

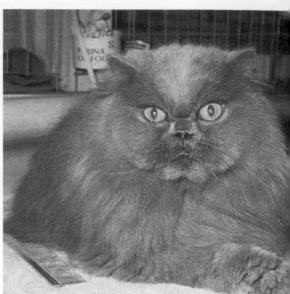

The white Persian cat has blue eyes. Black Persians have eyes the color of copper or orange. Blue Persians have deep orange eyes. All Persians have silky soft long hair and either blue or orange colored eyes.

The tortoise-shell cat has
patches of orange, black,
and tan fur. Its eyes are
dark orange.

Tabbies may be long
haired or short haired.
Long-haired tabbies may
be black, tan, or gray with
markings of spots or

stripes. Most tabbies have green or yellow-brown eyes.

Short-haired cats come in many colors. They may be all white, black, gray, orange, or red. They may also be multicolored with patches or stripes.

Above: Cats come in many colors
Left: Burmese kitten

Short-haired tabbies are almost always gray or brown with dark stripes.

A Burmese cat has a coat of dark cocoa brown with dark stripes. It is quiet and gentle.

31

The Siamese cat has short tan fur. Its face, ears, legs, and tail are much darker. But when Siamese are born they look almost white. All Siamese cats have blue eyes.

Siamese cat nursing her kittens

Siamese cat

Siamese cats are very active. They love to climb and jump. But Siamese are not very friendly. They take a long time to get to know strangers.

Some Manx cats might have a
stump, but no Manx cat has
a full tail.

A Manx cat may be
black, white, or almost any
color. Its hind legs are
longer than its front legs.
Also, Manx cats are born
without tails.

CHOOSING A CAT OR KITTEN

If you are going to get a cat or a kitten, get a healthy one. A healthy cat has bright eyes. Its fur is clean and shiny. It is playful and active.

Kittens need their mother's milk for the first seven weeks of their lives.

Don't get a kitten that is less than seven weeks old because it is not ready to leave its mother and her milk. Be sure to take your pet to an animal doctor right away. Kittens and cats need shots to keep them well.

FEEDING YOUR CAT OR KITTEN

Until it is about three months old, a kitten's stomach is the size of a walnut. It needs four small meals a day. Two may be just milk with some cereal. Two should be meat or fish from a can.

After your cat is three months old, you can give it three regular meals a day. At six to eight months, a cat is almost fully grown and should have only two regular meals a day. Always have a bowl of water for your pet.

Cats are very clean. Train your kitten to use a cat box filled with newspaper and litter or sand. Change the box often. Cats will not use a dirty box.

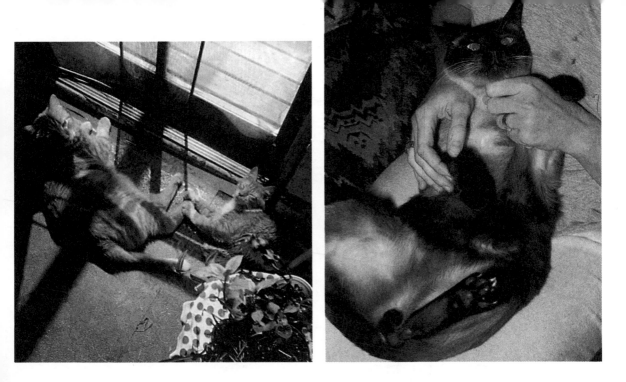

KNOWING YOUR PET

Cats like to sleep in warm sunny spots. Cats like to be petted and tickled under their chins and on their backs and tummies.

Some cats love to be picked up. Others may not like this at all. Cats will sit in your lap and play only when they want to.

Cats are very nosy. They will climb into paper bags, boxes, and open drawers or cupboards.

Like wild cats, your cat's
paws are padded and it
can move quietly. Most
cats have five toes on
their front paws and six on
their back paws. A cat
uses its front paws to
touch and feel things. Its
back paws are used for
fighting and climbing.

A cat's whiskers tell it
how far away a thing is,
whether it is soft, hard,
rough, or smooth. Whiskers
also help a cat find its
way in the dark and keep
it from bumping into
things.

A cat's tongue is rough.
It uses its tongue to clean

its fur. Many hairs stick to it and are swallowed. The hairs form a ball in its stomach and can make it sick. To help your cat, put one teaspoon of mineral oil in its food twice a week and the hair balls will not bother it.

KEEP YOUR PET
HAPPY AND HEALTHY

Don't handle kittens too much. Treat them gently.

Don't bathe a cat unless it has gotten into something terrible. Cats usually will clean themselves.

Feed your cat regularly. Keep its litter box clean. Brush its fur.

Be sure it gets exercise.

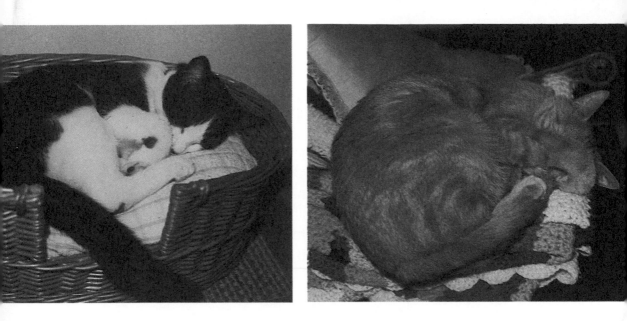

Give it a good place to sleep away from a draft.

Give it a fresh bowl of water every day.

Take it to the animal doctor when it is sick.

Love your pet cat and play with it.

WORDS YOU SHOULD KNOW

Africa(AFF • rih • ka) — one of the seven continents

Asia(AIJ • uh) — the largest continent on Earth

desert(DEZ • ert) — a place with little or no water

forest(FOR • est) — a place with many trees and other plants

jungle(JUNG • il) — a place that is hot and humid and has a thick growth of trees and other plants

litter — material that is put into the box which an animal uses for a toilet

mane — long hair that grows from the neck and head of some animals

Mexico(MEX • ih • koh) — a country on the continent of North America

North America — one of the seven continents

swamp(SWAHMP) — an area of soft, wet land full of mud

plains(PLAINZ) — large, flat area without any trees

Sibera(si • BEER • ee • ah) — an area in the northern part of Asia; part of the Soviet Union

South America — one of the seven continents

The Children's Reading Institute offers several card learning programs for development of reading and math skills. For information write to Children's Reading Institute, Drawer 709, Higganum, CT 06441.